Authentic Color Schemes for
VICTORIAN HOUSES
Comstock's Modern House Painting, 1883

Authentic Color Schemes for
VICTORIAN HOUSES
Comstock's Modern House Painting, 1883

E. K. Rossiter and F. A. Wright

DOVER PUBLICATIONS, INC.
Mineola, New York

Bibliographical Note

This Dover edition, first published in 2001, is an unabridged republication of the work originally published by William T. Comstock, New York, in 1883 under the title and subtitle *Modern House Painting: Containing Twenty Colored Lithographic Plates Exhibiting the Use of Color in Exterior and Interior House Painting, and Embracing Examples of Simple and Elaborate Work in Plain, Graded, and Parti-colors.*

Library of Congress Cataloging-in-Publication Data

Rossiter, E. K. (Ehrick Kensett), b. 1854.
   [Modern house painting]
   Authentic color schemes for Victorian houses : Comstock's modern house painting, 1883 / E.K. Rossiter and F.A. Wright.
      p. cm.
   Originally published: Modern house painting. New York : William T. Comstock, 1883.
   ISBN 0-486-41774-3 (pbk.)
    1. House painting. I. Title: Comstock's modern house painting. II. Wright, F. A. (Frank Ayers), b. 1854. III. Title.

TT320 .R83 2001
698'.12–dc21

00-065778

Manufactured in the United States of America
Dover Publications, Inc., 31 East 2nd Street, Mineola, N.Y. 11501

PREFACE TO THE SECOND EDITION.

THE authors are naturally gratified at being called upon to write a preface for a second edition of a work that seemed hardly qualified to survive the first thousand. In the work of revising the plates, they have borne in mind as far as possible the criticisms that have been made. Many things, however, had to remain as they were, unless, indeed, the book was to be made entirely new. The indulgent reader must admit that this would be too great a liberty to take with a publisher, upon whose stock of patience liberal drafts had already been made.

In the first edition care was taken to point out failings and shortcomings. This was done not for an appearance of frankness, or for the purpose of disarming criticism; if the plates were to be of use, according to the intent of the authors, as suggestions and guides for the inexperienced, it was thought wise to show wherein they ought not to be blindly followed, and wherein modifications might advantageously be made. It might be supposed that such a course would be unnecessary for a second edition. The new plates can, indeed, be commended as far excelling the first set. They are as satisfactory as can be reasonably expected. Still, there are errors, and in few cases are the plates just what was intended. Hence it is judged wise to point out defects and note improvements that might be made, as before.

Of the changes made, the most important are Plates I., V. and IX., which are substantially new plates, and are among the most satisfactory of the book. Plates II., VI. and X. are entirely changed in coloring, and many of the other plates have been modified somewhat.

June 1st, 1883, 149 Broadway, N. Y. City.

CONTENTS:

CHAPTER I.

INTRODUCTORY.

IN all departures from generally accepted standards, and in all innovations that embody anything of a startling nature, the radicals are the prime movers, and usually come to the front as the men of action, who inaugurate, and set in motion, the machinery designed to carry out the new idea. This, naturally, often results in extreme measures at first; but, afterwards there comes the inevitable conservative reaction which tends to moderation and temperance. That which the reform embodies of good is carefully garnered up, while that which is fanatical and meretricious is gradually sifted out, and rejected. The final working out of the new ideas may be said to result in neither the one extreme of radical innovation, nor in the other of conservative inaction; but in the golden mean between the two, which is tolerance within reasonable and well defined limits.

Some such process as this is at the present time being worked out in architecture. The present architectural renaissance of the so-called Queen Anne, Free Classic, and English Domestic styles, represents an important movement in the right direction, which has all the characteristics of a true reform. The renaissance of the architectural styles prevalent over a century ago is marked by efforts of a new and original nature, resulting in elaborate complexity, and wild vagaries, not strictly warranted by ancient authority. The movement is now fairly inaugurated, with all its inconsistencies, absurdities, oddities, and extreme fanatical tendencies, brought prominently to the foreground, in full accordance with the general law we have noted. The reaction has not yet set in, but already have been heard the mutterings which presage its coming, in the protests entered here and there against some of the more especially indefensible examples, and in the growing tendency to reject features which will not adapt themselves to modern exigencies and practical requirements. Some of the good features of the new style—features that have stood the crucial test of adaptability and utility—have also been recognized by this time, and have been unhesitatingly adopted as among the architectural ideas that will live. There has grown up with the present style, as indeed an integral part of it, an ever increasing demand for and love of color. The broken surfaces and picturesque outlines of the modern Queen Anne country house offer many advantages for almost endless artistic color treatment, not possessed by former types, and it is very gratifying to find that this is seen and appreciated. This is in itself one of the most important of the good results of the revival. Color bears such an intimate relation to it that, at the risk of having it considered somewhat out of place, we cannot refrain from broadly analyzing the new style.

This is the more necessary because of the very widespread ignorance as to what is, and what is not, real Queen Anne work. Any piece of modern work in which some old and quaint effect has been introduced, or in which some ancient detail has been copied, has been unblushingly christened Queen Anne. The name has been made to do duty for classifying any departure from ordinary and well accepted standards. Not infrequently we see two buildings whose characteristic features are diametrically opposed, classed as Queen Anne, when the truth is that neither of them partakes in any degree of what can strictly speaking be so designated. Modern Queen Anne, or Free Classic, is based upon English examples of domestic buildings erected during the reigns of William and Mary, Queen Anne, and the first two Georges, and also upon buildings of a later date of a nondescript character, which resulted from an exceedingly lively effort of an eclectic school of designers to break away from English Domestic Gothic. Drawing its features from so many sources, it is not easy to clearly define them. Generally speaking, however, they are such as result from the application of classical details to Gothic forms and mediæval principles of construction. The general form and arrangement of these buildings was after the Gothic manner: *i. e.* they were designed from the inside; the plan was the first consideration, and was made to meet the practical requirements of the times, while the exterior was left in a great measure to take care of and adapt itself to the plan. Breaking away from the bad precedents established by the Renaissance, especially the practice of subordinating the convenience of plan and interior effects to the requirements of a classical exterior, symmetry began to be considered as no longer the all essential characteristic of good architecture. Picturesqueness was aimed at and, while the claims of convenience and utility may have been often sacrificed to whims and quaint conceits, yet, in general the result was an advance beyond the elaborate baldness of the Palladian class of renaissance buildings which were at one time becoming very numerous. The new school of designers was, and is now, eclectic, claiming the right to use the special features and details of any and every style, which can be bent to harmonize with the requirements of their buildings. The tendency is to substitute for the heavy and clumsy Gothic detail, the more delicate, graceful, and refined features which characterize the renaissance of the Grecian and Roman styles. There are strictly speaking but two great styles of architecture, the underlying principles of which are based upon the construction. One is the classical style, based upon the lintel as its chief constructive feature, and the other the mediæval Gothic in which the arch is used to span openings. Modern styles are chiefly the result of a compromise between these two great systems. They are transitions from one to the other in which characteristic features of both are blended.

The prototypes of the present style in England were generally executed in brick or stone, and for real Queen Anne these are the materials required. Our country houses are for the most part of wood, and in working out the problem of keeping to the essential features of the style while the material is different, many modifications of old, and new features have resulted. Colonial architecture affords many examples in wood which take the place of brick prototypes. The differences between colonial work and contemporaneous Queen Anne are such as arise chiefly from their being worked out in different materials. In the better class of Colonial houses these differences are more marked. In some of these examples the symmetrical planning is evident, and they partake of the classical idea more than of the Gothic. They are very valuable for the detail which they con-

tain, and much of the best in modern work is drawn from this source.

Modern Queen Anne, using the term to cover in a general way all the present reigning styles, is founded upon these various examples in our own land and abroad, and thus partakes of the characteristics of many local styles. In its better phases, however, it is very different from its prototypes, being marked by greater freedom of treatment, and being broken up more in outline and form. The detail has also undergone considerable change. Greater refinement, richness, and delicacy of expression, has been attempted, than in the old examples, and the result is, perhaps, a more harmonious whole. A modern style must reflect modern tastes and modern ways of life, and it must fail where it attempts to copy the old without regard to adaptability or fitness. It is in this respect that the extreme of unreasonable fanaticism is reached.

Modern styles cover a wider range, and embrace a larger school of purely eclectic designers than ever before. They have not yet crystalized into any very definite forms. They are respectively called Queen Anne, English Domestic, Colonial, or Free Classic, as the different supposed characteristics of these various styles are thought to predominate, but they all elude any definite architectural analysis. Things are in a state of transition, for the most part. Buildings that are recognizably definable in any distinct style are rare. It is, perhaps, well that it should be so. There is no good reason why we should not learn all that we can from the past, and recall from oblivion all that is good and adaptable to modern life. This is what is now taking place, and it cannot be denied that our houses are, in consequence, gradually assuming a more homelike and picturesque character much to be preferred to the manufactured style so monotonously prevalent at one period.

If for nothing else, let us be thankful for the opportunity offered for better color treatment. Exterior house decoration has been obliged to keep pace with the new ideas, and effects which do not admit of commonplaceness in coloration. The old puritanical hatred of color, which found its natural outcome in white houses with green blinds, has had to give way; at first, to a compromise, in which neutral and sickly drab tints played a prominent part and, later, to more advanced notions, in which the more positive colors find a chance of expression. The old rule, which only allowed two colors to be used on the exterior of a house, one for body color and the other, a shade darker, for the trimmings and blinds, is undergoing modification, and numerous exceptions are being taken to it. The present style of architecture does not oblige its enforcement, but rather tempts to the use of more colors and a diversified treatment. Where the lines and surfaces are so much broken up as they are now, the old ideas are, indeed, out of place, and cannot rigorously apply. The use of shingles for covering wall spaces, exterior paneling, and the treatment of gables, offer many advantages for coloring never given before. But behind the opportunities thus afforded lies an awakened love for color itself, the sense of which has only lain dormant. Much has been written that has tended to stifle this sense. Real positive colors have been thought to be inharmonious with the quiet and subdued tones of northern landscape, and hence condemned. Cold, grey, neutral tints and light drabs have been urged as the only kind of colors that go well with surrounding landscape. The result has been that violence has been done to nature by glaring effects and contrasts that are hideous. There is no good reason why a house, no matter what its surroundings, should not be gratifying to one's sense of color. It is well that a certain fitness of things should obtain, but this is not incompatible with the use of as much real color as individual taste may desire. Positive colors, if not too harsh, but mellowed and softened down in hue, or dulled in tone, will be found to harmonize with natural objects as well as anything distinctly artificial can, or ought.

There are a great many attempts of the new school, which, in coloring and combination of colors, are miserable in the extreme. This is only natural, and to be looked for. Yet already, notwithstanding repeated failures and absurdities, good is being felt, and we find that real progress has been made, such that at no distant day we are lead to believe that our villages and towns will be dotted with attractively painted houses—houses which are gratifying to our sense of color, and which will always convey a certain pleasure when looked at.

There seems to be an earnest desire on the part of the people at large to fall in with the new ideas, and improve the coloring of their homes. This is noticeable in the widespread inquiry in relation to new methods of house decoration, and the reception accorded every publication on the subject. The few isolated examples of parti-colored painting in some of the seaboard towns, that a few years ago were looked upon as startling innovations, are no longer considered as such, and people are now, with more or less success, engaged in copying what has been done, or in trying to get something of like character. Many who want to do what will be considered in good taste are puzzled to know what colors to use, and how to direct their painter so as to give him a tolerably clear idea of what they want. For all such our colored plates will, perchance, be found of use. It is believed that there is a demand for a book of this kind, and that even if the results set forth by the plates may not be exactly what each individual reader would choose, it will be of benefit to both the painter and the house owner as a partial guide. It is put forth, not as containing things which should be directly imitated, but as pointing out some of the methods of the new school, and as illustrating, as well as the art of chromo-lithography will permit, some of the newer ways in which a house may be decorated.

It may be well to note that the colors obtained after the plates had passed through the hands of the printer, varied considerably from the original designs, and in few cases are they just what the authors had in particular view. The difficulties in the way of getting the colors right in the printing are as great as getting the colors right on the house. Even with the colors placed before his eyes, the printer as well as the painter often fails to match the desired tones. The results, however, are sufficiently near the originals to convey the meaning intended, and will answer, at any rate, as practical suggestions to all who choose to avail themselves of them.

CHAPTER II.

COLOR.

THE limit and scope of this work forbid any extended treatment of the subject of color, a subject, be it said, that has suffered too much already from incompetent handling to be lightly undertaken. Those of our readers who expect to find lists comprising all the various scales of color, giving definite information as to what particular color should be used to harmonize with this or that shade, and telling just what combinations are allowable, and just what are to be condemned, will, therefore, be disappointed. Something of this sort will be attempted in outline, but it is not intended to lay down definite rules for the guidance of the novice; such rules would be apt to prove as confusing as they are sometimes misleading, for the subject does not admit of exact prescription. It is best that the element of individual taste should have plenty of room for exercise, governed only by that sense of the fitness of things which limits all originality and prevents violence being done to well accepted canons. We are more concerned that the results themselves should be plainly set forth, with simple explanation of the means and a few of the underlying principles, than that a treatise should be presented with complex investigation as to *why* certain combinations are pleasing, and *what* are the scientific relations of one color to another.

We are far from asserting, however, that study in this direction is useless. It has undoubted value in determining many points, but it can never quite supply the lack of a natural taste, or "good eye for color." An investigation of this kind, leading to formulas applicable to every case, may prove of benefit in educating the taste to a certain extent; but, after all, it is the fine, innate perception of color, conceived without reference to any particular rule that reaches the most satisfactory results. The great difficulty in the way of furnishing a formal set of rules that will be of value lies in the fact that no two persons have precisely the same idea of the same color, and that there is no absolute standard to which appeal can be conveniently taken. The variations of hue, tint and shade are indefinite for each color and all its combinations. How difficult, then, must it be to satisfactorily write an alphabet of color, that will enable the uncultivated eye to grow into a knowledge of the fullness and richness of the language!

It is just as difficult to deal with the practical side of the question as it is with the theoretical. A rule prescribing the various quantities of pigments that enter into the composition of a given tone, must, of necessity, presuppose pure materials; but pure materials are not to be uniformly obtained. In fact, they are the exception and not the rule. Perhaps, four times out of five, the material will be highly adulterated, and a formula for mixing, which is based on the pure article, would, of course, give far different results with adulterated pigments. The proportions must be altered to suit the special impurity, and nothing but a trained eye to perceive the right degree and intensity of the color sought will answer. For these reasons, it will, perhaps, be better for us not to attempt what, from the nature of the case, must lead to uncertain results; but to confine ourselves to.a discussion of general principles, pointing out the path that leads in the right direction, trusting to the general good taste of the individual reader to follow it to good advantage. At the outset, it may be well to glance at the generally accepted classification of colors, with incidental comment and definition.

The primary colors are Red, Yellow and Blue. They are called primary because, in theory, all other colors can be obtained by combinations of these three, while they themselves are impossible to compound by mixture of any other colors. There seems to be some doubt about Yellow, some maintaining that it is a compound of Red and Bluish Green. It is certain that Yellow could never be compounded of Red and Bluish Green *pigments*. Maxwell, in his celebrated theory of color, gives Red, Green and Blue as the primaries, and Helmholtz asserts that Red, Green, Blue, Yellow and Violet should be so considered; but these theories treat of colored rays of light by spectrum analysis, and not especially of the mixed pigments that we have to deal with. The Red-Blue-and-Yellow theory is the common and popular one, and more nearly correct as regards colored pigments.

Secondary colors are so called because they can be theoretically obtained by mixing any two primaries. There are three secondaries, Green, Orange and Purple. The following table will show how the primaries combine to form them:

Yellow added to *Blue* gives *Green.*
Yellow " *Red* " *Orange.*
Blue " *Red* " *Purple.*

As to the relative quantities of the combination, no rule can be given. Yellow in 3 parts will perhaps combine best with 5 parts of Red and 8 or 9 parts of Blue.

The Tertiary colors comprise all the other colors that can be obtained by combination. They practically include almost every color in use. They are called tertiary because, from a theoretical standpoint, they are obtained by mixing any two secondaries. Hence there can be but three Tertiaries. They are Russet, Olive and Citrine, obtained as per the following table:

Orange added to *Purple* gives *Russet.*
Green " *Purple* " *Olive.*
Green " *Orange* " *Citrine.*

Just what proportions of the secondaries should be used, in order to produce the tertiaries, cannot be given. There is a good deal of uncertainty about *Russet, Olive* and *Citrine*, as, indeed, about all tertiary colors. The primaries and secondaries can be fixed more easily, and agreed upon; but few people will be found who can unite upon one Olive, for example, as the representative Olive. Some writers say there are six tertiaries, viz.: *Olive, Russet, Citrine, Buff, Plum* and *Sage*, on the theory that tertiary colors ought to be considered as nothing more than the dulled tones of the primary and secondary colors. Others, on the ground that all colors must be classed as tertiary which are neither primary or secondary, hold to, and proceed to define, a still larger number of colors of the third class. This theoret-

ical disagreement is of little practical importance. It is best to adhere to the simpler classification. We shall then have nine namable colors in all; three in each class, viz.: Red, Yellow and Blue in the 1st Class; Green, Orange and Purple in the 2d Class; and Russet, Olive and Citrine in the 3d Class. These may be, for convenience. termed the positive or normal colors.

White and Black ought not, strictly speaking, to be regarded as colors. Mixed together they give Grey, and these three are sometimes called the neutral colors. White and black are also known as *extreme* colors, as, according to optical analysis, all other colors lie between, and approach them in their various tones from light tints to dark shades. It will be simpler not to consider them as real colors, but to assign to them their office of producing the different scales, of which every color may be said to have three, obtained by modifying it with White, Black and Gray, respectively.

In order to better understand what is meant by a scale of color, some preliminary definitions are in order:

A *Tone* of color is obtained by mixing any normal color with either White or Black in infinite variety of proportion. A *tone* comprises both a *tint* and a *shade*, *tints* being the result when the normal color is mixed with White, and *shades* when mixed with Black. It is important that the difference between a *tint* and a *shade* should be clearly understood. A *hue* of color is produced by modifying one normal color with another. It will be seen that each color, in its various compounds of shade and tint, is capable of almost infinite variation between the two extremes of Black and White, When the shade is very dark, the color approaches Black, and when very light, White. The variation of hue for each color is limited only by the number of colors.

A *Scale* is a regular series of *tones*. Each color admits of three scales, viz.: 1. The *Reduced Scale*, consisting of the various tints of the normal color, obtained by mixing it with white. 2. The *Darkened Scale*, consisting of the various shades of the normal color obtained by mixing it with Black. 3. The *Dulled Scale*, consisting of the various shades of the normal color obtained by mixing it with Grey. Grey is defined as a combination of Black and White.

Besides the classes of colors above mentioned, viz.: Neutral,

Primary, Secondary and Tertiary, reference is sometimes made to a fifth class, called semi-neutral colors, of which Brown and Grey may be taken as examples. The classification into neutral and semi-neutral is of no especial importance, save that it is sometimes convenient to so designate them.

This may conclude the outline of the subject of color classification. It contains what every man who paints should know concerning the theory of colors. It would be well if every one, both of the profession and laity, knew this much of the subject. For those who may wish to learn more, we would mention the following books, which treat of the various theories, and much other related matter:

"Grammar of Ornament." By Owen Jones. An expensive work; perhaps the best book on the subject. Of more use to the decorative painter than others; but containing much on color, and fine colored plates which in themselves are an education.

"Grammar of Coloring." By G. Field. An important work, and perhaps of more special value to painters than the "Grammar of Ornament."

"Color." By A. H. Church. A small, inexpensive work, with concise statement of the various theories, more especially relating, however, to colored rays of light than to pigments.

"A Manual of House Painting," etc. By Ellis A. Davidson. Containing, besides the theory, much of practical importance on every question that a house painter is interested in, such as the properties and uses of colors, and how they should be prepared, mixed and applied.

"House Painting," etc. By J. W. Masury. A small book, containing advanced ideas on the subject of painting which every painter should be aware of.

"Haney's Painters' Manual." A very useful little compendium of everything connected with the trade.

"How to Paint." By F. B. Gardner. Contains much useful information that is intended to make "every man his own painter."

Other works going into the subject at great length, in a purely scientific way, are:

"The Laws of the Contrast of Color," by M. Chevreul; Dr. E. Brücke's Treatise on "Colors;" papers on the subject by Dr. George Wilson, Helmholtz, and Professor Clerk Maxwell; and two works by W. Benson, entitled "The Principles of the Science of Color" and "A Manual of Color."

Other works might be mentioned, but these will amply suffice to choose from. To the professional painter such a work as Davidson's, for instance, which treats specifically, and at some length, of the technical part of his work, is almost as necessary a part of his stock in trade as his brushes and pots.

Every painter, who makes any claim to be abreast of the times, owes it to himself and to his patrons to be well informed as to the properties of the various colors, and how to mix them to secure a certain desired result. He should know all about the various processes of painting, and the principles which govern them; all about the special treatment suited to each particular case; and all about the physical properties of every material he has to deal with. He should know what colors are best in respect to lasting powers, what colors fade out quickest, and what colors will withstand the fierce rays of the sun; and, generally, he should be posted on everything that is known concerning the special preparation and use of color. We have a right to expect this much; but, as a matter of fact, our expectations are rarely realized. Very few of the craft have an intelligent knowledge of that which it is their business to know. The study of the subject, from its theoretical side, is almost entirely neglected when the practical part is so easy to acquire, and the consequence is endless disappointment at the hands of those on whom most people depend for the coloration of their houses. Special directions are of little value when there is no theoretical knowledge of the primaries which enter into the composition of any desired color. Without this knowledge the painter's work is nothing but a matter of experiment, and liable to result in something far different from the color desired.

Returning now to our summary of color classification and combination, let us note what use can be made of it. First, however, it will be necessary to deal with the terms "complementary," "contrast," and "harmony."

A complementary color is defined to be the color which, with the color of which it is the complement, makes up the three primaries. Given, any color or colors, their complement or complements consist of the remaining color, or colors, that constitute the primaries, or equivalent proportions of them. A few examples will enable us to understand this better. The complementary of any primary color is a combination of the other two primaries. For instance—

The complementary of Red   = Yellow + Blue = Green.
  "   "   Blue   = Red   + Yellow = Orange.
  "   "   Yellow = Blue + Red   = Purple.

Note that the secondary colors are the complements of the primary colors, and *vice versa*. The complements of tertiary colors are not so easy to determine. The best way to do so is to consider them as merely dulled tones of the primaries. The complementaries will then be dulled tones of the secondaries. For instance, Citrine may be considered as nothing more than the primary Yellow, dulled with Grey = a Yellowish-Grey. The missing primaries here are Blue and Red = Purple, and Purple-Grey (known as Plum Color) is the complementary sought. In the same way, considering Russet as nothing more than Reddish-Grey, and Olive as Bluish-Grey, the complementaries are, respectively, a Greenish-Grey (known as Sage) and an Orange-Grey (known as Buff). As for the complementaries of other tones and hues, they can be found in the same way; but it is not easy to determine them by rule. A very good and simple way of finding the complementary of any color whatever, is to take a piece of paper about two inches square, tinted with the color whose complementary it is desired to find; lay it down on a piece of white paper and look fixedly at it for a moment or so; then withdraw the colored piece, still continuing to look at the place where it lay, and the complementary color will appear on the white paper, either as a fringe of color around the edges of the square where the color lay or as a solid square of color, occupying the same position on the white that the original color had. This simple method may be found of use in determining those colors which cannot easily be analyzed. With some people it does not work as well as with others, and with all it requires a quick and observant eye to accurately note the complementary, because it vanishes in a second. This experiment, it may be well to note, is a good practical illustration of the intimate relations of colors to each other, and of the way they mutually affect one another.

A contrast of color is simple or compound. Each of the primaries forms a simple contrast to the other two. Thus, Red forms a simple contrast to Blue and to Yellow. A compound contrast to Red would be Blue and Yellow mixed, which is Green—in other words, the compound contrast of any color is the complementary of the color. This is the strongest kind of harmonious contrast that can be made. Simple and compound contrasts are contrasts of color and hue. Another kind of contrast is that of tone, every variation of which forms a contrast with the normal color, and every other variation. This is the more important kind in relation to house painting. The laws of contrast, and the way that colors mutually affect one another when placed in juxtaposition, to be satisfactorily treated, would require more space than the size of the present work allows.

We shall allude to them hereafter, and incidentally touch on the subject again in the plate descriptions.

Harmony of color consists in the preservation of the same character throughout. The various hues and tones used must have a subtle relation to each other—a relation that is seen and felt, but which is not easily described or predicated. We shall refer to this part of the subject elsewhere, and in connection with the plates.

What can be learned from the theory we have outlined is relative rather than absolute. The theoretical combination is very rarely the actual. But, notwithstanding these drawbacks, a knowledge of the theory cannot fail to be of advantage to every one. It shows at least in what direction our efforts should tend, though it leaves much to individual taste and caprice. The choice of color, indeed, should reflect a certain amount of originality of taste, where there is an almost infinite number of colors to choose from. Choice is only limited by questions of durability, cost, and facility of mixing and combining. When we come to speak of the colors by their commercial names we shall have something to say concerning the colors which will last longest.

The general principles that relate to the theoretical outline we have been considering are few, and may be mentioned briefly, to conclude our chapter on color.

Avoid using any of the primary colors in the pure state. They are all too positive and intense. If used at all, they should be used as sparingly as they are exhibited in nature—only to pick out and emphasize certain kinds of ornamentation. This holds true of almost all the normal colors. They are best when toned down and modified in hue.

The "*darkened*" or "*dulled*" scales of color are to be preferred to the "*reduced*" scale. For house painting, as a general rule, pure tints, unless they have considerable depth of color, should be avoided. The tones of any color produced by combination with White alone, are apt to be weak and sickly in expression, as well as glaring in contrast with the landscape. Modern improvement in painting houses began with tints of a pale and delicate tone, which took the place of the almost universal white house and green blinds. Another step in advance is marked by the present taste, which inclines to stronger and more robust tones—tones that contain as much real color as may be craved; but never of a positive kind—always dulled and softened down to reasonable harmony, so that the eye seeks them with pleasure, and does not weary of them. These rich, and sometimes sombre, colors give a house a certain character and dignity, which the washed-out looking light drabs and lavenders generally fail to produce. Modern taste of the best kind does not seek for exciting effects, for decided hues, for glare, and for obtrusiveness; but for results which will be restful; for softness of color, and for that subdued and quiet expression which should characterize the exterior of every house in which refinement is supposed to lodge.

A knowledge of the color complementaries is a great help in the choice of color, where any wide departure from monotone painting is undertaken. In looking at any color, the eye naturally seeks the harmonious contrast of its complementary. Great care must be taken that the complementary shall be of the same tone as the color, as otherwise discord will follow.

Harmony of color is said to result when the three primaries, either in the pure state, dulled, or in their various combinations of secondary or tertiary colors, are equally distributed. This does not mean that, for instance, Red, Yellow, and Blue should be present in equal *quantity*, but rather that the *quality* of the whole shall partake of the three in proper proportion. This is a principle that is true within such a very wide latitude, that it scarcely admits of practical application. One application would lead to the use of complementary colors to a greater extent than is perhaps desirable. As a matter of fact it is the trained eye which alone can best determine whether there is balance, or equal distribution of color in any composition. Harmony is something which transcends the power of any rule to define. The best general direction for securing it is, perhaps, as follows:

In general it may be said, that if a number of colors in combination contain a common ingredient, and are sufficiently influenced by it to be drawn to one another, a certain harmony is sure to follow. For example: a shade of Red may be placed by the side of a shade of Yellow, without the least resultant harmony; but, if some Yellow be introduced in the Red, or some Red be introduced in the Yellow,—which amounts to the same thing—the Red and Yellow will immediately have a certain affinity for each other. This is the principle which may be said to govern the production of harmonies of tone and hue,—harmonies that are much easier to obtain, and perhaps more suitable for exterior house painting than the powerful contrasts of complementaries. Treatment on this principle may often result in both harmony of tone and harmony of contrast, which is, of course, very desirable. For instance, take the complementaries Red and Green. They may be so toned down with Grey that the complementary effect is not lost, while the Grey is present in sufficient quantity to be noticeable in its office of modifyer. Any number of colors can be subjected to this principle. Frequently, a number of colors, which are exceedingly discordant, when looked at through a colored glass will be found to harmonize perfectly. This may be taken as a practical experiment, going to prove the desirability of a common color entering into, and running through the whole, in order to bring about a unison of effect. The binding of colors together in this way is nothing more than giving them *tone*, and when colors *tone* well with each other, the result is harmonious. It is so with musical notes. They must accord, or tone, with one another or there is no harmony. Music and color are intimately related, in that they both depend on harmonious combination to produce a good effect. If they fail of this, the result is discordant. Just here note the difficulty of prescribing rules that will answer. Color taste is like musical taste, a matter of education and slow growth to most people, and as with music, so with color, the taste for the highest kind is formed, by hearing in the one case, and seeing in the other, the best examples afforded.

It may be well before closing to allude to the terms "cold" colors and "warm" colors. Colors are called cold or warm because of the corresponding sensations they are supposed to excite. Of the primaries, Yellow is classed as a warm color, and Blue as a cold color. Red is not so warm as Yellow, and by some is held to be neither warm or cold, but a happy medium between the two extremes. Generally speaking, however, those tones in which Yellow and Red predominate, are known as warm tones, and those tones in which Blue takes any prominence, as cool tones. Contrast of tone is always the strongest when a cool color is contrasted with a warm one, and when strength is sought, this is the way to get it.

If what has been said on the subject of color is sufficient to awaken an intelligent interest in the mind of the reader, the purpose of the authors will have been fulfilled. In subsequent short chapters we shall touch on the more practical side of the question.

CHAPTER III.

PREPARATION, USE AND APPLICATION OF COLORS.

WITHOUT going into minute detail, we propose to jot down in this chapter, under general heads, points that relate to the more practical side of the question. Bear in mind that the information thus to be given is intended for all classes,—not for painters alone. Also it is intended to apply to the exterior, unless otherwise mentioned. We shall not appear as advocates of any new technical manipulations, or trench upon things that lie within the painter's own peculiar province. The experience of practical men, upon many points of technique and handling is, and from the nature of the case must be, the only safe guide. We shall speak from the architect's standpoint, and in general try to give just such information as we would judge to be of value to any of our clients should they ask our advice.

PREPARATION.—The fresh wood should be thoroughly dry and free from dust. Our preparatory application, to be of real service as a preservative, must enter into all the pores and interstices of the wood. It is obvious that it cannot do this if the pores are full of dampness. The oils, which are the vehicles by which paint is applied, cannot mix with water and cannot displace it. Any moisture in the wood will surely act as a disintegrating force to any paint that may be applied. Another source of disintegration is the sap or gum resin. New pine always contains more or less of this, even after considerable seasoning. The sap in solution will certainly destroy the paint. How to prevent this, is an important question. There is no available remedy. It has been recommended that the wood to be painted be exposed to the action of the weather forces for one season,—i. e. through one summer and winter—before being touched. This would cure the evil undoubtedly. The action of the weather would bring out of the wood the substances injurious to paint, and besides it would roughen and harden the surface so that the paint would have something to cling to. But this is not an available remedy. We cannot expect people to live in unpainted houses for a year, even when it would lead to their final benefit. The usual practice is for the painter to follow the carpenter, and it must be submitted to notwithstanding its attendant evils. We can only look to it that our wood is tolerably seasoned and tolerably free from sap and knots. If the wood be then fairly dry, and certainly free from moisture and dust, we shall get the best results that the circumstances admit of. There are always more or less knots to deal with. Here is where the most trouble is experienced, on account of the sap which will sooner or later exude in spite of any known preventive. In the interior, where the powerful rays of the sun have no chance to act, the difficulty of sap and knots is not so great. The usual course to pursue in regard to knots is to give them a coating of shellac varnish. This is the best thing that can be done. There should be two coats, one applied after the other is dry. This should be done before the priming is applied.

PREPARATORY COAT.—Crude petroleum is one of the best wood preservatives known. It has been tried conclusively and found very beneficial. Its use has been endorsed by the Government. We would recommend its application as a preparation for the priming. To a certain extent it can even take the place of priming. Wood, when treated with petroleum, will take the paint better and cause it to adhere longer. Being very thin, it penetrates into the wood deeply. It fills the pores and interstices, and in every way serves a good purpose. It is very cheap ; a barrel of it costs something less than five dollars, and will cover all the exterior and interior wood work of a moderate-sized house. It can be applied with a cloth or large brush, and rapidly put on. Painters generally do not concur in what we have said concerning the advisability of preparing by a coat of crude petroleum.

PRIMING COAT.—This is the ordinary first coat of paint ; usually composed of white lead and oil. The special purpose of the priming coat, when there is no other preparatory coat, is to fill the pores of the wood and in general to prevent the absorption of moisture and the consequent shrinkage. To a certain extent it does prevent subsequent shrinkage, but not altogether. There is nothing that will wholly arrest this. In regard to the priming coat we beg to offer the following advice: It should be thin, and well rubbed in. Do not use white lead alone unless the final color is to be white; let the base be something that will give a darker color than the final color desired. It is always best to work from a dark color up to lighter ones. The color of the priming should be very nearly that of the finishing coat. The priming coat is best considered as a stain, composed of linseed oil and turpentine with the color used instead of a base.

PUTTYING.—After the priming is dry, all nail holes, cracks and defects should be filled up with putty composed of linseed oil and whiting. The putty should be colored when there is to be but two coats. It should be applied with a knife—never with the fingers.

FINAL COATS.—Good work requires at least two coats besides the priming. When a preparatory coat of crude petroleum is laid on, two coats, one of which is the priming coat, will answer. The third coat can be put on after the house has stood for one season. This is a very good plan. If the colors should prove unsatisfactory, they can then be changed. Each coat of paint should be thoroughly dry before its successor is applied. The paint should be laid smoothly, be uniform in color, and even in thickness.

STAINING.—The difference between a stain and a paint proper lies in the absence or presence of a *base*. Paint is composed of a *base* consisting usually of white lead, red lead, or zinc white, mixed with a *vehicle* which is usually linseed oil or spirits of turpentine, and the *coloring pigment*. In some cases the *coloring pigment* answers as a *base*, but generally speaking the colors are too expensive to be so used, and all coloring pigments are not adapted for such use. A stain has no *base*. It is simply the *coloring pigment* applied to the wood by means of any *vehicle* which will hold the color in solution. A stain has not the body that paint has, owing to the absence of a base, which is what gives paint its body and covering-up property. A paint covers and lies on top of the surface of the wood. A stain goes into the wood and does not hide the grain. The wood remains the same as it was before, only darkened and colored.

The large use of shingles for covering the walls of modern houses has led to the adoption of staining the exterior when so treated. Formerly it was only the wood of the interior that was stained, it being thought that stains on the exterior would not stand the exposure to the weather. This is true, and constitutes at once their greatest merit and defect. The weather acts on a stain to wash out the color. All colors are more fugitive when used as a stain than when they are employed as paint, and for this reason it is best to use more of the color. It will fade into lighter tones. This is the objection to staining on the exterior. It is also a merit, for this weathering process results in new tones and softening effects that it is impossible to get with ordinary paint. The stain does not fade out entirely. In some places the color will be darker than others, and the result is a diversity of shades that as a rule harmonize well with each other and go a great ways towards relieving the monotony that usually obtains with a painted surface. For exterior work the best way to apply a stain is through the medium of turpentine and linseed oil. The mixture of the color and oil should be thinned with considerable turpentine, so that it will strike in the wood. The turpentine aids the color to penetrate, and the oil serves to hold it. The surface should then receive two coats of oil. It is thought best by some to apply the stain with turpentine only, and then add the oil in separate coats; others hold that no turpentine should be used. The important part is to get the color well into the wood and then provide to keep it there. If this result can be brought about by using other mediums than oil and turpentine, as the individual experience of the painter may certify, the conditions of a good stain will have been fulfilled. Vinegar is sometimes used as a vehicle for staining, and gives good results. The mistake usually made is in the non-application of after-coats of oil. Thoroughly good work requires at least two coats of oil on top of the stain. Frequently when it is not desired to change the natural color of the shingles, two coats of oil with the color mixed in will suffice. Sometimes the shingles are dipped in oil before they are put on the house. This answers very well with shingles of California red wood, when it is only desired to bring out the natural color, but even with these shingles it is best to give them an additional coat of oil after they are up. We have seen shingles that have been stained and oiled, treated with a final finish of varnish, with the idea of holding the color. This it will do, but aside from the expense of such treatment, the gloss that varnish gives is not desirable, and it takes away from the soft graded coloring that is the peculiar charm of stained shingles.

It should be noted that there is more or less uncertainty involved in staining or painting shingles. The final effect, with inexperienced hands, is generally different from what was intended. It depends a great deal on the manner in which the shingles are laid. The same paint or stain gives different effects, according as the shingles are laid in straight courses with square ends, or with the utmost irregularity. Shingles are now laid on so as to break up the surface very thoroughly with touches of shadow, as, for instance, when shingles of different lengths are used, or when the ends are cut in different shapes, or when they are laid in wavy lines. On the same house all of these different kinds may be employed. The result is a great diversity of color effect, which is greatly to be commended. The use of shingles which have a very rough surface—ordinary sawed shingles—gives effective and artistic results, as some parts of the shingles with the roughest surface will catch more of the color than other parts, and great diversity of color is thus obtained. The uncertainty of the result need deter no one from staining. If the stain is properly applied and well oiled, the final effect will be found soft and agreeable, even though it be different from what was intended.

READY-MIXED PAINTS AND COLORS.—From an architect's standpoint, the objection to ready-mixed paints is that the colors are not what he would in most instances choose. Some of the paints manufactured by responsible houses are all that they claim to be—pure lead and oil; but a ready-mixed paint should be avoided, unless from a responsible house. One's choice is limited to comparatively few colors, and often undesirable ones, although there are houses that compound colors on special orders to match any desired shade. In regard to the various patent and chemical paints with which the market is flooded, it is enough to say that few of them are fit to be used for exterior work. There is nothing better than linseed oil and pure white lead for painting, and the introduction of lime, soap and water certainly cannot add to their good qualities. As to colors ground in oil which come ready for use, they are probably better ground, and, generally speaking, the chances of getting an adulterated article are no

greater than if the painter should buy the dry colors and grind them himself. On the whole, our advice to the painters would be to get the very best materials; avoid adulterations; the best is the cheapest.

ESSENTIAL QUALITIES OF A GOOD PAINT.—It should have a good body, or the property of covering up. It should be such that it will flow on easily with a brush, adhere to the surface without running, and leave coats of equal thickness when the surfaces are inclined or even vertical. After it is applied it must become hard; that is, it must dry out and harden. After hardening, it must be capable of adhering to the surface firmly. And, lastly, it must be durable. It is seldom that any paint combines all these good qualities, and a paint cannot approach them unless the materials are pure and unadulterated.

DURABLE COLORS.—A very important question to be answered with reference to every color, either when used alone or in combination with other colors is, how will it stand the rays of the sun and the severe weather of winter? Many colors, when used singly, are unchanging, but when combined with other colors they cause the resultant color to fade or turn dark. Generally speaking, the manufactured chemical colors will not answer for outside work, and chrome yellows, chrome greens, Prussian blues and American vermilions are fugitive either singly or in combination. The ochres, stone-yellow, Indian and Venetian reds, burnt and raw umbers, and burnt and raw siennas are good and reliable colors. It may be well to go into the subject of fugitive and non-fugitive colors more in detail, and also to incidentally note other properties of the various colors of commerce. For trade purposes the coloring pigments may be grouped under the following heads:

White,	Red,	Yellow,	Blue,
Black,		Brown.	

All tints, shades and hues may be obtained from the above by admixture.

Whites.—White lead is the body color for all tints, and should enter to some extent into all paints to give them body. The common adulterations are barytes, whiting and silicate of potash. Zinc white has less body than white lead, but it is more durable. Especially is this true on the sea shore, where zinc white should always be used in place of white lead. The salt air acts injuriously on white lead. Zinc white is more delicate and whiter than any other white that can be used for exterior work. These are the only whites that should be used on the exterior.

Blacks.—Lampblack and vegetable black. Both durable.

Yellows.—Chrome yellow, King's yellow, and Chinese yellow are fugitive. Yellow ochre, stone ochre and Naples yellow have a good body and are durable.

Reds.—Venetian red, light red, Indian red and madder lake can be depended upon, but carmine, lake, vermilion and chrome reds are best avoided on the exterior, if permanent results are desired.

Blues.—The only blue that will stand is ultra-marine, and this is too expensive for house-painting purposes. Some of the imitations are said to answer very well. Prussian blue, cobalt, Antwerp blue and indigo will fade either singly or in combination.

Browns.—Raw and burnt umber, raw and burnt sienna, burnt ochre, purple brown and Van Dyke brown are all permanent colors. Raw and burnt sienna are sometimes classed as yellow.

In the chapter on color we advocated the use of hues and shades in preference to tints. White lead and zinc white should, in following out this idea, be used sparingly. The color itself should form the principal body or base. This is a most important thing in connection with modern house-painting, where it is desired to obtain real color in all its richness and transparency. The thing of most importance in any paint is the oil, and most of the essential qualities of a good paint lie in it and not in the bases themselves. Dryers, and solvents, and bases we must have, as well as proper manipulation, but, after all, it is raw and boiled linseed oil that accomplishes the result of preserving the wood and holding the color.

The Plates

PLATE I.

A PRETTY little gate-lodge or small cottage might admit more vivid and brilliant coloring than a more pretentious and dignified building, especially if it be surrounded by trees, or if it has a background of foliage of some sort. For, in painting any house, one of the things to be borne in mind is evidently its relation to surrounding objects. The house should be related to its surroundings in much the same way that a picture should be related to its background—the wall it hangs on. It is not always easy to judge whether the setting will admit of high coloring. If the cottage shown in this plate was hidden in green foliage, through which only occasional glimpses of it could be had by the passer by, brighter colors might be allowed. Here, however, we have imagined it well on the road, where bright colors would be unduly conspicuous. The owner, who with very quiet tastes nevertheless loves color, will do well to follow the scheme here shown. The color on the shingles could not, perhaps, be obtained by staining, although a near approach to it could be had with Indian red as a base. If paint is used the shingles had best be first dipped in crude oil or painted one coat before being put on. Else when the shingles shrink under a hot sun, as they are sure to do, a crack will exhibit the unpainted surface. Besides this, the paint would form ridges at the bottom of each course, catching the water and thus hastening the decay of the wood.

The trimmings throughout are in a green complimentary to the red, and the body color of 1st story is in a rich brown. The roof is slate, and the blinds might be a dull red.

Rossiter and Wright, archt.

PLATE II.

THE trimmings of a house are usually painted in a darker color than the body, the idea being, no doubt, that those parts of the house which denote in some measure its construction, should be emphasized in painting. But, a great deal that a painter is apt to deal with as "trimmings" is anything but constructional in character, and should not be emphasized from any point of view. Take a house, for instance, devoid of anything but vicious ornamentation—gimcracks and stuck-on ornaments bearing no relation to the construction. Here, if the painter is left to follow the rule, the result will be an enhancement of the defects, for the very things that it would be good taste to screen as far as possible by uniformity of one color, will only stand out more prominently.

Outside of such considerations there is no very good reason for following any rule in regard to trimmings and body color. In this plate the trimmings are made a lighter color, and the body colors are dark. The effect of a house painted after the scheme shown here would be extremely rich and elegant, much more so in reality than the plate shows.

Trimmings, sepia, Indian red and white. Body color, first story, mineral green, blue-black and stone ochre. Roof, blue-black and yellow ocre. Body color, second story, a shingle stain of burnt sienna, Indian red and brown madder Blinds, green in second story, red in first.

Rossiter and Wright archts

PLATE III.

THIS is an attractive combination of colors, and cannot fail to be pleasing if satisfactorily executed. The trimmings approach the tertiary color citrine— *i. e.*, a normal green, toned down with black and white. The white is assumed to be present in all these mixtures in the shape of white lead or zinc white. The green, like all other greens to be used on the exterior, can be obtained from blue, black, yellow and red. The exact proportion of course cannot be given. Nothing but actual experiment will suffice to determine the color. This is merely one shade out of an infinite number that can be obtained by various proportions of blue, black, yellow and red. The panels in the gable pediment and those along side of the hall windows of first story are painted a shade of Venetian red. (Venetian red, black and white). The pine shingles of second story are to be stained, two coats of burnt sienna, with burnt umber in it, the resultant color being a rich yellowish brown of a very pleasing nature. The body color of first story may be considered as a darker shade of the second story color, approximating closely to the tertiary russet, with the red in predominance. The colors used to compound it are Indian red and burnt umber. It should be dulled with but very little black and white. It will be noticed that the scale of color is what we have elsewhere spoken of as the dulled scale. It is necessary that the darkened or dulled scales be used where the normal colors are brought into play, as they are here. The roof is not shown in color. If it is a shingled roof, it can be painted red or stained a reddish brown. In most localities, at the present time, it is almost as cheap to slate a roof as to cover it with shingles. We have hence assumed that in all the larger houses the roof would be covered with slate.

Outside blinds would appear best if painted the same shade of dulled Venetian red used in the gable. They may also be painted the russet of first story with good effect.

PLATE III

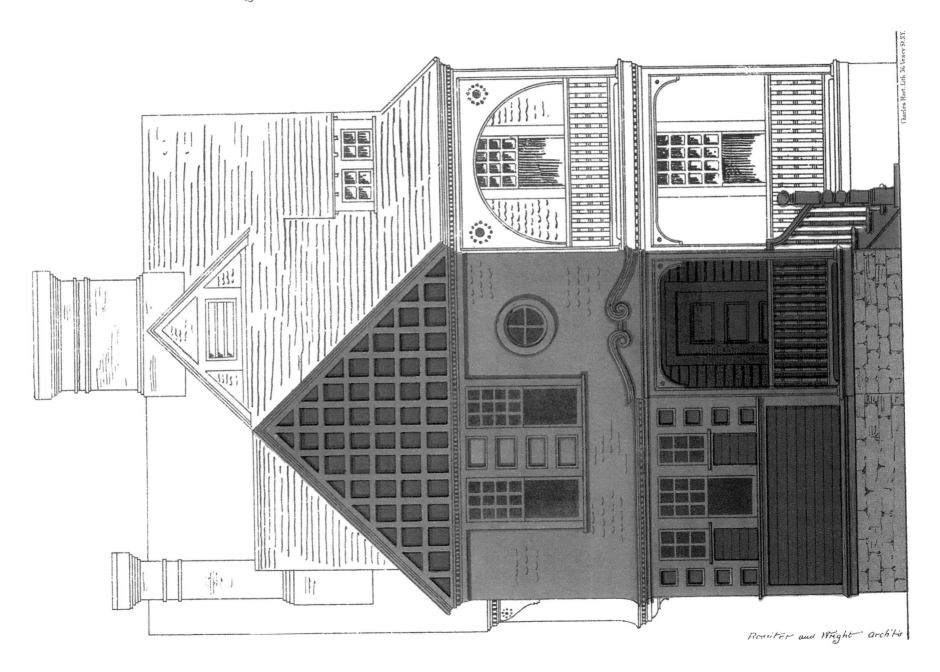

Rositer and Wright arch'ts

PLATE IV.

THIS design is presented as a fair example of a modern Queen Anne wooden house. It may stand as a type for houses of a more expensive nature than the designs given in the foregoing plates, and, as far as the painting is concerned, it will answer as a guide for all houses where there is a large use of shingles. The decorative idea underlying the painting as shown in the plate, consists in grading the colors from heavy rich shades at the bottom, up through a middle harmony to the lighter tones of the gable peaks. The tones used for this purpose are warm and rich. The trimmings on the contrary are painted a cooler color, giving great strength of contrast, and emphasizing the body colors. The roof would, perhaps, be of slate. If it was covered with red tiles, the effect of the whole would be improved. The blue-grey of the trimmings would bind the other colors better if it contained more red than it does. Blue-black and Indian red will give it. The yellow of the gables is nothing but a dulled stone yellow, mixed with very little black and white. The middle tone is very nearly like that shown in plate III. It is really a lighter tint, brought about by using less of the burnt umber. Referring to plate III., it will be seen that this color is obtained by a repeated stain of burnt sienna with burnt umber in it. The gables (stone yellow) are also to be stained, two coats to insure the color. The gable peaks of the porches of first story give good opportunity in this design to break up the color effect by bringing the three graded tones in close juxtaposition. The body color of first story is painted. Colors used are Vandyke brown and yellow ochre, with a trifle of Indian red, and dulled with a little black and white. A building of this class ought not to have outside blinds. The arrangement of the windows is such that outside blinds cannot open without shutting against other windows. The ordinary inside blind would be better, and best of all the Venetian blind. If outside blinds should be used they had best be painted a color that closely approaches the middle tint, and also the body color of first story. In other words, the color should be a darker shade than the middle tint, and lighter than the body color. This color may be obtained by using burnt sienna and Vandyke brown, dulled with white and black.

In regard to the appearance of this plate, the authors are confident that those who love richness and warmth of color will not go wrong to take it as it stands for a guide in painting designs of a similar character.

PLATE IV

Rossiter and Wright arch'ts

PLATE V.

TRIMMINGS, Van Dyke brown and Indian red.

Body color, brown madder, yellow ochre and white.

Roof, a slate color, shows rather too green in the plate.

Blinds in body color.

The two colors here combined can be highly commended. Such colors are not alone applicable for a pretty little cottage. Almost any variety of house, large or small, would look well in them, and the effect would be rich and dignified. The combination is an example of harmony of tone; on the whole, the safest and best kind of harmony to seek after in exterior painting.

PLATE VI.

TRIMMINGS, Indian red and Van Dyke brown.

Body color of first story, Indian red and brown madder.

Body color of second story, a light stain of brown madder and yellow ochre.

The roof was intended to be painted a blue-black and yellow ochre green, but as printed it is rather too pronounced, and there is a Prussian blue constituent in it, which is, of course, always to be avoided for exterior work.

Leaving the roof out of consideration, the scheme of color is a good one. The dull red of the first story is a fine color, and the contrasts afforded by the lighter trimmings and still lighter second story color, are both striking and pleasing.

Rossiter and Wright, Arch'ts

PLATE VII.

TRIMMINGS, Indian red, blue-black and stone yellow.

Body color of first story, sepia and Van Dyke brown.

Body color of second story, mineral green, blue-black and stone yellow.

Blinds should be same as the second story color. If the roof is of shingles it would look well in a reddish brown color, Indian red and burnt umber mixed.

The color on the stone foundation is not exactly true. It ought to have been a dark grey. Foundations, however, can generally be left to take care of themselves. If they are of good stone they should not be touched, and if they are in brick, the best thing to do is to give the bricks two coats of oil with perhaps a red stain.

The body color of first story should have been a green several shades darker than the second story. The brown is rather strong and inclined to give a dingy effect.

PLATE VII

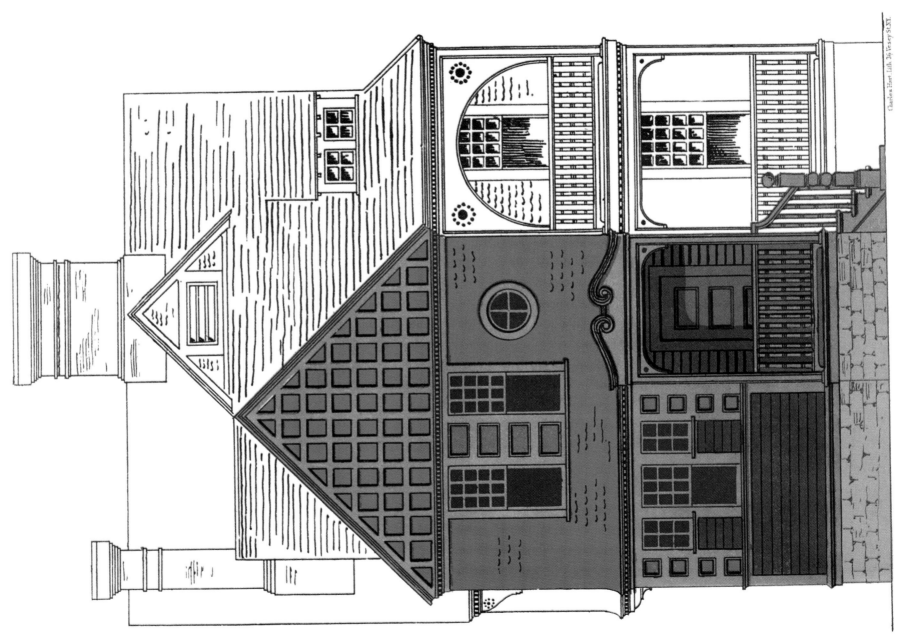

Charles Hart Lith. 36 Vesey St. N.Y.

Rossiter and Wright archits

PLATE VIII.

TRIMMINGS, brown madder, black and white.

Body color of first story, sepia, blue-black and yellow ochre.

Body color of second story of the same ingredient, with the addition of mineral green.

Gable shingles stained with chrome-yellow and Indian red.

It may be that the painter will prefer to obtain the colors we have shown in these various plates by compounding with colors different from those mentioned. The same color can frequently be obtained in two or three ways. Care only should be taken to exclude those colors from the combination which are of a fugitive nature. If this is done, and the painter can match the colors by other mixings, there can be no objection to his doing so.

There is a fifth color shown in the panels—a mistake that must be attributed to the printer. The panels had best be in the body colors.

This plate is another example, like Plate IV. of the same design, of a treatment in which the colors are massed and graded. The authors do not believe in the practice, which obtains to a great extent lately, of picking out small members in a brighter color than the rest, in order to enliven the whole. This gives a building a choppy and mincing effect, and instead of bringing out and helping the architectural design in a subordinate way as color should, it is apt to result in undue emphasis of features which ought to be kept back, and to give other parts a relative importance that is far from desirable. Let it be borne in mind that color is chiefly important in architecture as an adjunct of form, and that it can never quite take the place of form. On the exterior, color can properly emphasize form, but it should never be used so that it interferes with picturesqueness of outline and refined detail. We refer more particularly to the custom of painting chamferings, mouldings and ornamentation in a positive color—frequently a bright red. These features in a design ought to be appreciated in light and shade only. They bring out the form in detail, and the emphasis of shadow is quite good enough without recourse to more violent methods

Rossiter and Wright archt's

PLATE IX.

TRIMMINGS, yellow ochre, gamboge and black. Body color of first story, mineral green and black. Shingles of second story, a stain of burnt sienna and white. Roof shingles, Indian red. The gable panels are in rough cast plaster. Blinds, same color as first story body.

This would be an effective and bright composition for a small tree embowered cottage ; the contrasts of color are strong, but being in the dulled scale they are not too striking for this kind of a design. On a different kind of a building it might not answer at all.   It must be borne in mind that all buildings can not be treated alike. The colorings that with some designs would be very effective, on others would be out of keeping. The fact is that a house should be painted so that its salient features of form and detail will be enhanced.   The coloring should be subordinated to the design.

PLATE IX.

Modern House Painting.

A 1881

Charles Hart. Lith. 36 Vesey St. N.Y.

Rossiter and Wright arch'ts

PLATE X.

THE prevailing russet shown here can be obtained by a mixture of Van Dyke brown and Indian red—as a stain on the shingles of roof and walls and as a paint for the body color of first story. The gable shingles are painted green (mineral green and black) in harmonious contrast to the other color, and the trimmings are made to harmonize in tone with the body color. The color can be had by mixing Indian red, sepia and white. Blinds should be green. The foundation is shown in green. It would be better to leave it in natural bricks, oiled.

The effect of a stain and a paint is quite different, even though precisely the same colors be employed. Hence the shingles, which are shown in the plate the same as body color of first story, would not really appear the same. The surface of the material has a great deal to do with color effect. If the surface is rough or much broken up, the effect will he different from the same color on a smooth and uniform surface.

Rossiter and Wright Arch'ts

PLATE XI.

TRIMMINGS, blue-black and white. Body color of first story, sepia, and yellow ochre. Shingles of second story, stain of burnt sienna and Van Dyke brown. Blinds, Indian red.

This is one of the plates that the revision has not only not improved, but has made much worse than it was before. As it is now there is little to commend. It is only fair that the authors point at what the intention was. The second story shingles should be a deep stain of pure burnt sienna, with the gable panels a lighter shade of the same color. The body color of a first story should then be a dark red—Indian red, Van Dyke brown and black. The trimmings should be a blue-black and yellow ochre green, complimentary to the red.

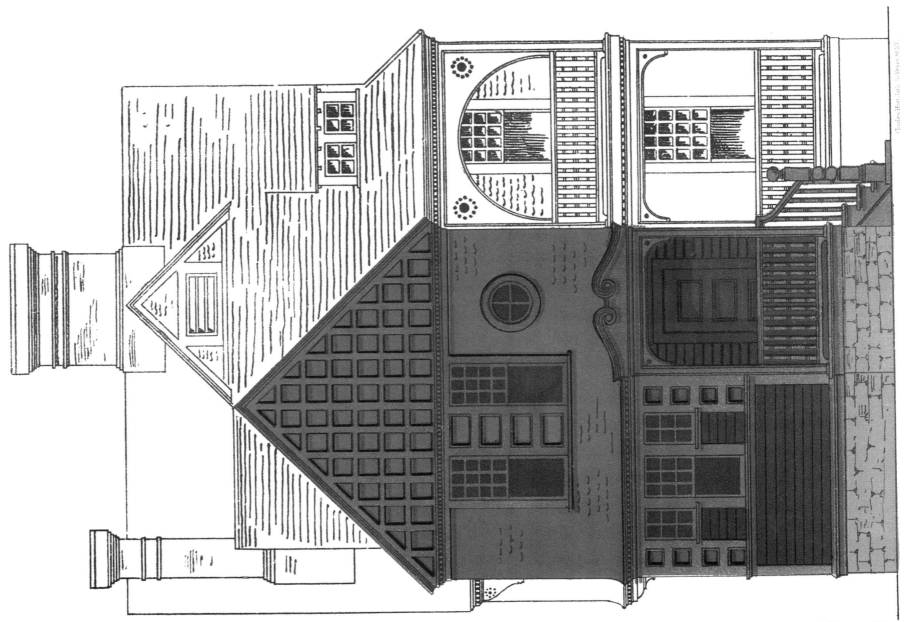

Rossiter and Wright arch'ts

PLATE XII.

THIS is a very good example of the harmony of tone elsewhere spoken of. The same color enters as an ingredient in all the colors, and the result is that they all have an affinity for, and are naturally drawn to, each other. The gable peaks are treated with brown madder and blue-black mixed with white. It will be best to add a little Indian red. The fine, rich hue of the second story can be obtained by staining the shingles two coats of brown madder and burnt sienna. It may also be obtained in painting by adding a little white and black to the madder and sienna. The body color of first story is obtained by mixing VanDyke brown and burnt umber with a little brown madder. The trimmings are here painted in harmony of tone with the other colors. In plate IV. the same design was shown with similar warm, rich body tones in strong contrast to the cool color of the trimmings. In this plate there is a different treatment, the trimmings being as warm as the body colors, and the contrast throughout is the contrast of tone, than which nothing can be more pleasing. The color of the trimmings can be obtained by mixing sepia and Indian red with white, the result being a tint. It would be a pity to have outside blinds enter into this composition, for it is very well balanced as it now stands, and the addition of large masses of another color, involved in the blinds, would not help it and might be detrimental to the general effect. If, however, they are a necessity, they had best be painted a color that will grade between the body colors of first and second stories. The addition of some VanDyke brown or burnt umber to the second story color would give the proper color.

Rossiter and Wright Arch'ts

PLATE XIII.

So far, we have been considering the painting of new houses, or, at least, houses that are modern in style. To give our book as wide a value as possible, we have introduced a few examples of houses of an older and, at one time, very numerous class. Houses such as these have to be repainted now and then, and in many parts of the country they are still being built. How to paint, is just as important a question in relation to them as it is in more modern houses, and there is need that they should, as far as possible, be painted in good taste. Two designs are shown; one, the typical French roof house, and the other a story and one-half gabled cottage, also typical of a very large class. Only a portion of each house is shown; just enough to properly indicate the painting. Designs like these do not lend themselves so readily to rich coloring. There are no shingles that can receive stains, and sombre colorings that are in place on other designs would here produce a heavy and unwieldy effect. Especially is this true of the French roof design. The cottage can receive freer treatment.

On this plate we have used tints of a medium depth. The body color of the French roof and the upper story of the cottage can be obtained by mixing burnt umber and Indian red with white lead, and is a neutral tint of considerable warmth. The trimmings of the French roof design and the body color of the cottage can be obtained by the same mixing, more of the umber and red being used, and less of the white. The blinds and sash are painted a compound of Indian red, blue-black and burnt umber. The colors for the body and trimmings might with advantage be deeper than is exhibited in the plate. This could be done by using large proportionate quantities of the umber and red.

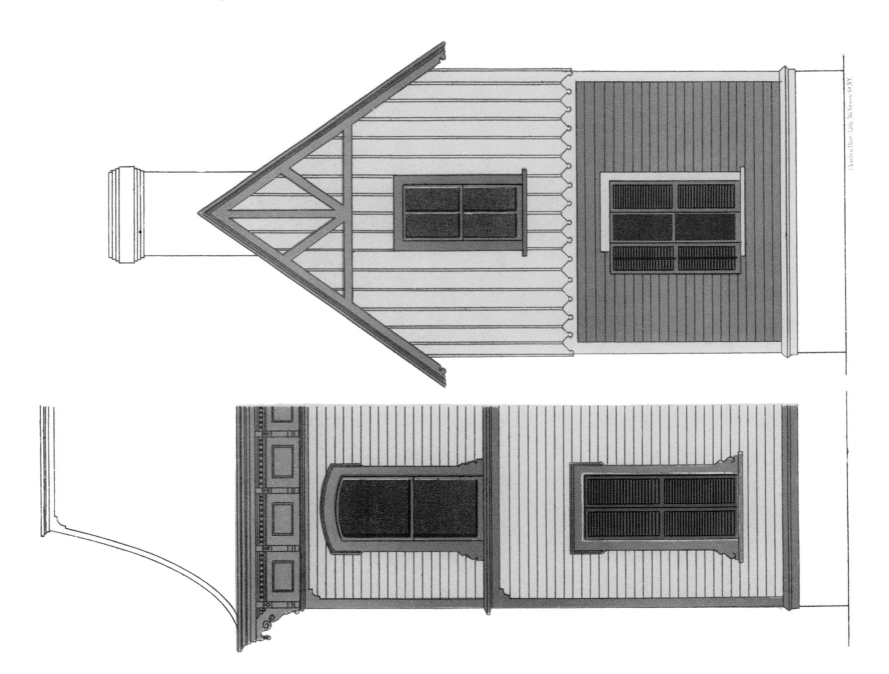

PLATE XIV.

THE coloring on the cottage here shown is an unusually good one for this class of building. Most people would probably concede this. It will not be so readily agreed, however, that the French roof design is happily painted. It would help one, who disagrees with the propriety of such painting, to appreciate and understand it better if they could see the house actually painted. We have known of not a few who, when these plates first appeared, came to us with expressions of positive disapproval, afterwards admit that the colorings "grew" on them, and many have experienced a complete conversion. To most people, both the ideas about colors and the colors themselves that are here set forth, are entirely new. Like all other new things they have to make their way slowly against old-fashioned customs and pre-conceived ideas.

The brown color is simply VanDyke brown, with a little white. The red can be had from VanDyke brown and Indian red, and the green is obtained from blue-black and yellow ochre.

PLATE XIV

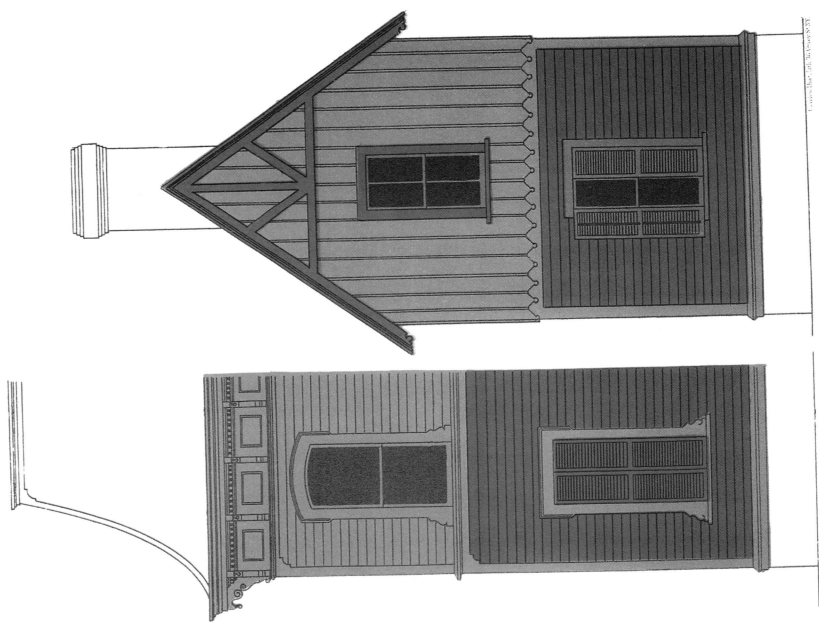

PLATE XV.

TRIMMINGS on French roof house, yellow ochre, gamboge and black ; body color, mineral green and black. Body color first story of cottage, sepia and yellow ochre. Second story color, burnt sienna and white.

Here again exceptions must be noted. The second story color of cottage is a rather raw contrast, and would look better if made the same as the trimmings of the French roof house. The body color of first story also is not quite as it should be. It is now too dark. The colors need more of the yellow ochre, and less of the sepia.

As to the French roof house, there may be some who will fancy the peculiar combination of green and yellow as it now stands. For our part we should prefer to see the green a trifle duller, using more of the black.

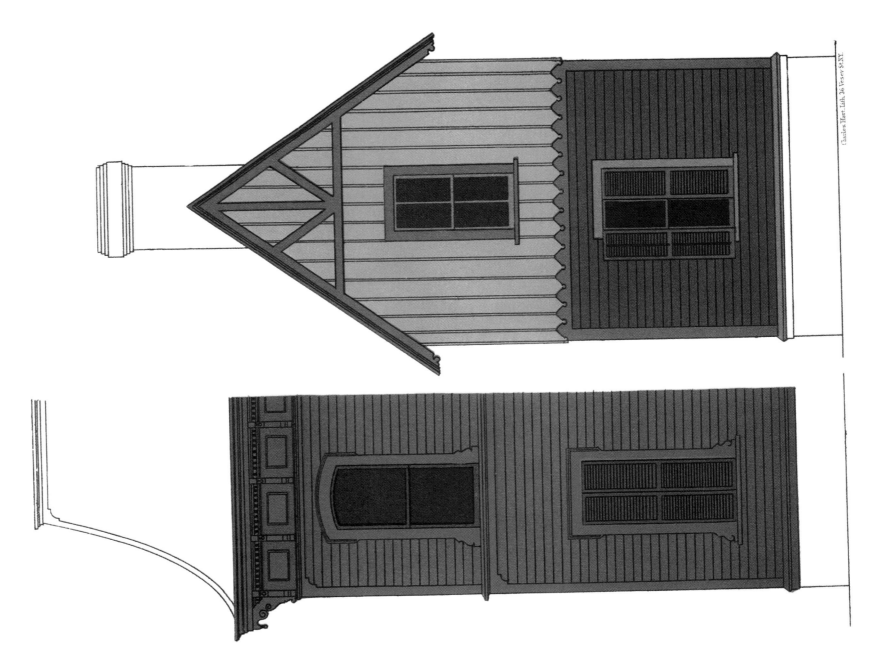

PLATE XVI.

IT has been thought best to introduce a few plates by way of illustrating the interior application of paint upon wood-work and wall surfaces. The subject is one that demands more attention than we can here give it, but as the object of the work is to treat more particularly of exterior painting, we may be excused from dealing with the matter in any other than in an incidental way. Interior house painting, of course, calls for the solution of the same problems that are to be met with in outside work. The exercise of good taste seems, however, to be even of more importance, from the fact that all interior painting assumes a more decorative character than that which is done on the outside. When we come to treating the inside of our dwellings, we do with almost a new feeling of color, for we must be governed by our surroundings, and a sense of fitness much more here than on the exterior. Paint when used should be applied with reference to what is likely to go with it, *i. e.*, the wood-work, doors, etc., should all be treated in connection with the wall and ceiling surfaces, so that a harmony of color will prevail throughout. The various rooms of a house should be painted, papered or kalsomined in such a way as to give each a distinctive character. The scheme of color used for the living-room should differ essentially from that of the bed chambers, boudoirs, etc., and while a richness and quietness of effect should be sought in one, a cheerful and sunny appearance should be aimed at in the other.

In the example before us, the wall color is a combination of Naples yellow, gamboge and white. The dado is obtained from Prussian blue and yellow ochre. The color would be improved by the addition of a little black, which would give what is known as "peacock blue." The frieze, formed by placing the picture moulding below the cornice, is in the same color as the dado. The wood work is meant to indicate any red stained wood—cherry, mahogany, or pine. As it is painted, however, it is a color which only could be had by painting with a mixture of Indian red, Van Dyke brown and white.

PLATE XVII.

THE same design as the last plate, the coloring differing chiefly in the wall color, which is here in a cool gray instead of a warm gray. The color can be obtained from black, white and gamboge. The woodwork is painted a mixture of burnt sienna and yellow ochre. It will be noticed that the panels are laid in a shade darker than the rest of the woodwork. This always has a good effect, and is one of the simplest kinds of decoration.

The plates may serve as color schemes for selecting paper, as well as guides for painting and kalsomining. The decorative principle as far as color is concerned, that should not be lost sight of, is this : darker colors should prevail at the bottom, lighter ones at the top. That is : the dado should be darker than the wall surface. It is evident that the reverse of this would produce a top-heavy effect. In regard to selecting papers after the colors here given, it may be well to note that the color shown should represent the background of the paper and not the figure. There are a great many wall papers with a dark background, and the figure or design in a lighter tone of the same color. A very good and harmonius result will always be obtained, when such a paper is used, by having the *background* of the wall paper the same color as the *figure* of the dado.

Rossiter and Wright archi'ts

PLATE XVIII.

THERE are many inexpensive and tasteful ways of painting a hall, and an effort should be made to render this portion of the house as attractive as possible. It is the part that one sees first upon entering a house and the last to be seen as one leaves it, therefore the importance of creating a favorable impression. The walls may be treated in an infinite variety of ways—may be either painted in cool colors or in warm ones, but a richness of effect should be aimed at. This can only be obtained by employing colors of considerable body and brilliancy. We have, in this plate, illustrated an inexpensive method of wainscoting in which the whole credit of effect is due to paint. Narrow strips of pine about one inch and a half in width and seven eighths of an inch thick are framed and planted on the wall. A cove moulding added forms a regular panel effect. The plaster panels thus formed are painted a Pompeian red—a mixture of yellow ochre, Venetian red and vermilion—and the panel frames, door and window trim a greenish drab, formed by mixing Van Dyke brown, yellow ochre and a little blue-black together. There is a slight greenish tinge given to the wall, which might with advantage be increased in depth. These colorings may serve as a guide for papering, which, if done, will greatly enhance the effectiveness of the decoration. The same colors are used in the cornice as in the wainscoting.

Rossiter and Wright architts

Charles Hart Lith 36 Vesey st N.Y.

PLATE XIX.

THIS plate shows another treatment of the same Hall design. The result is not as satisfactory as we would wish, but with a slight modification in the ingredients of the paints used, an effect more pleasing would readily be obtained. We would suggest that the green, in which there has been used some Prussian blue, be dulled with a little brown so as to give it more of a grey look, or, Van Dyke brown might be used without any other color, with a decided improvement upon what is presented. The salmon wall tint should not be so decided as shown, the introduction of more white would improve it. The panels are painted a light shade of Pompeian red, obtained by adding more of yellow ochre to the Venetian red and vermilion than in the preceding example. The door frame is in a lighter shade of the green.

PLATE XIX

Rossiter and Wright Arch'ts

PLATE XX.

THE painting of ceilings is a branch that stands somewhat apart from what is termed house painting. The subject is pursued in the main by specialists, and calls for a different class of work from what house painters attempt. It is, moreover, done in a different manner, and with different materials, though oil colors are frequently used ; yet, in the greatest amount of work, kalsomine and water-color fresco are given the preference on account of their cheapness and variety of tints. There is a softness and mellowness about work done in water-color fresco, that oil paint, even when flatted with turpentine cannot give, hence its very extensive use. Ceilings as now designed, offer an excellent opportunity for color treatment. In general, the largest surface should be treated with the lightest color, which may be of blue, buff, grey, or broken with any color that is thought desirable. The shades should be delicate and airy in tone, and the darker colors should arrange themselves in successive gradations of strength, the darkest and strongest color of all being in the cove of the cornice. The center piece may repeat the cornice colors, but should be less rich, as its isolated position would tend to render, it too conspicuous. The ceilings in this plate have the appearance of being somewhat too sombre—this is due to the fact they are seen entirely by themselves, and not with their proper surroundings. The furniture, carpets, window hangings, etc., would all have a tendency to relieve and lighten them, which they much need. Cobalt, black, and yellow ochre will form the grey that is used, and sepia, black and white, with yellow ochre, the buff. Van Dyke brown with Indian red is used for the outer member.

PLATE XX

Rossiter and Wright arch'ts